Max Jum

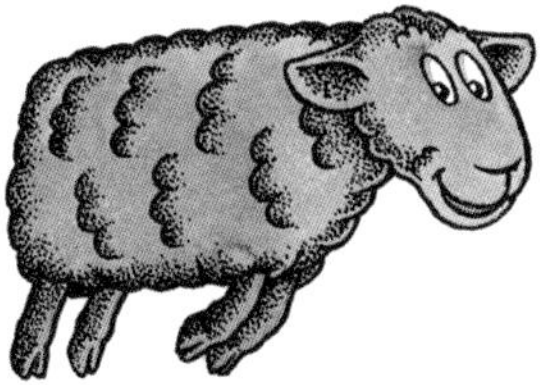

words by Nigel Croser
illustrated by Neil Curtis

Max jumps over a flower.

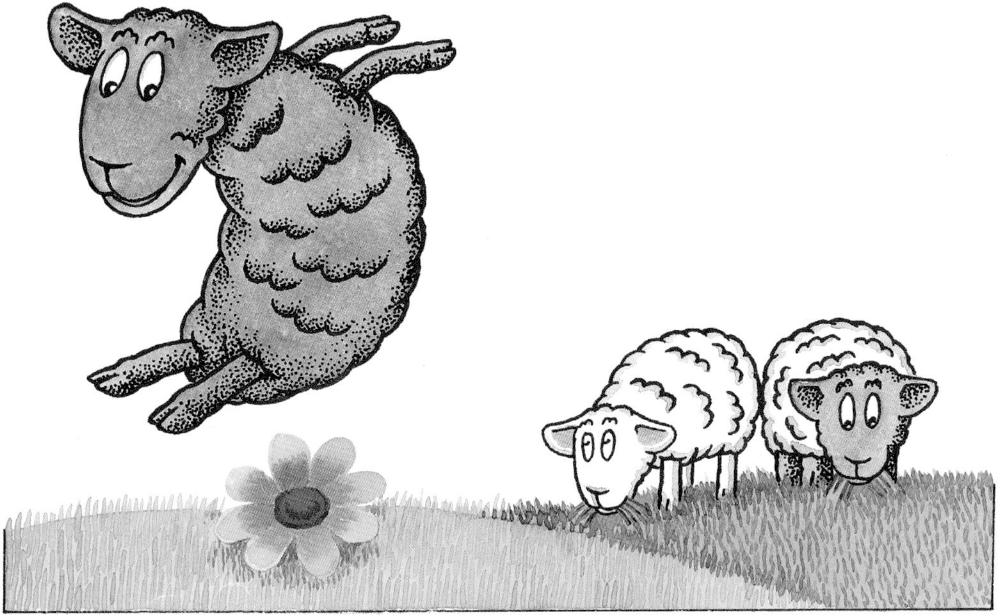

Max jumps over a stick.

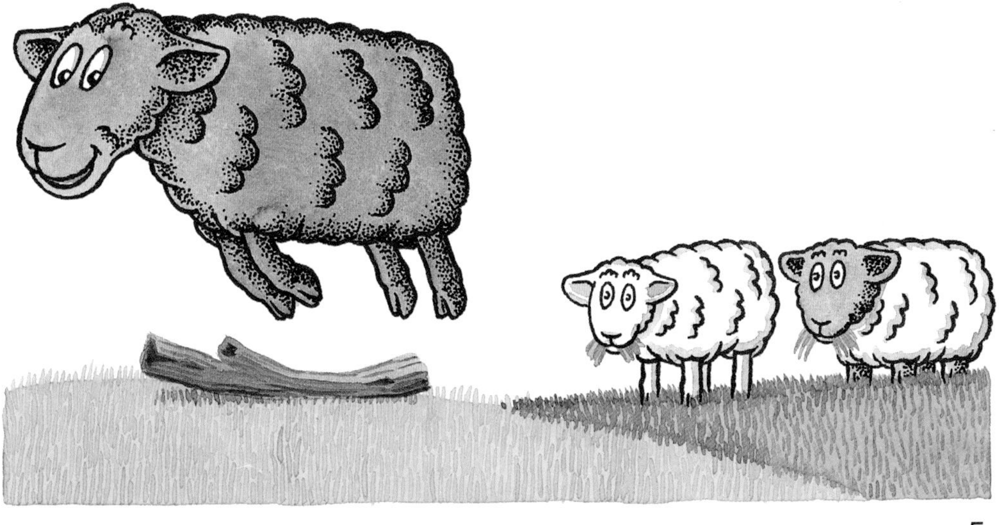

Max jumps over a rock.

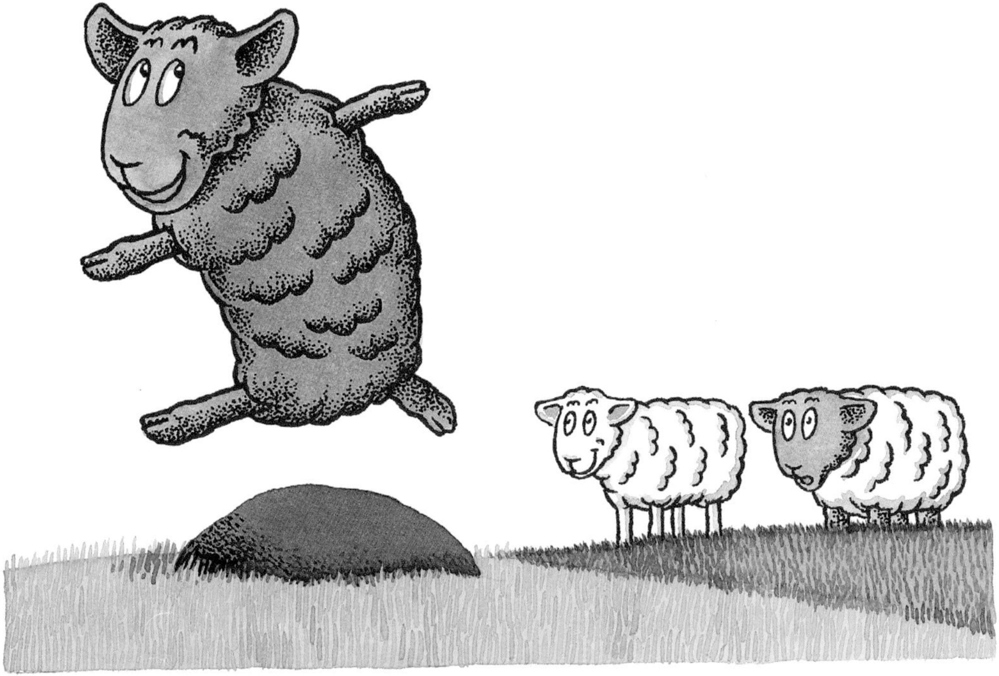

Max jumps over a log.

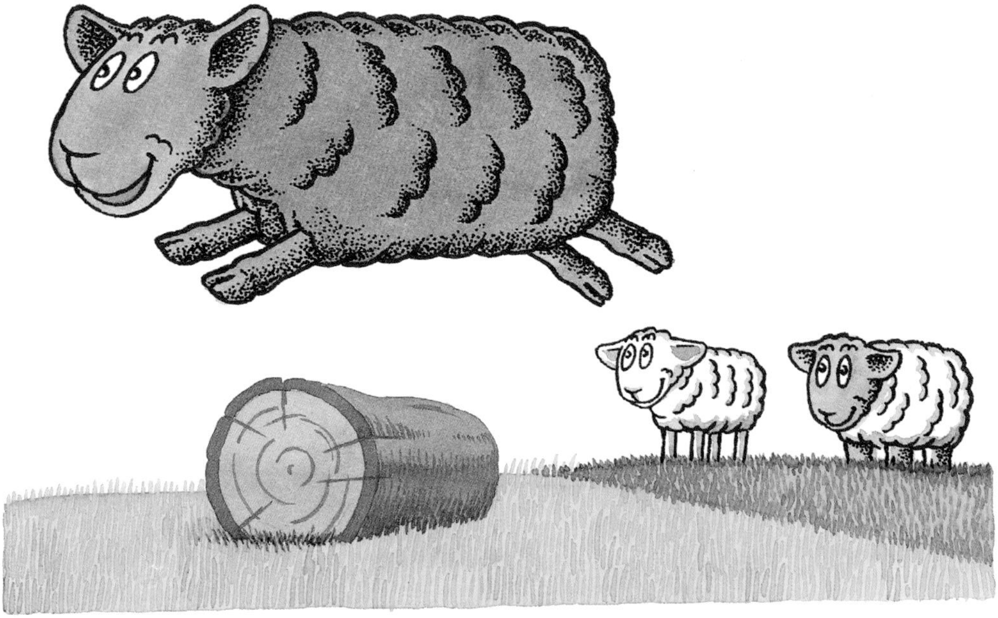

Max jumps over a bush.

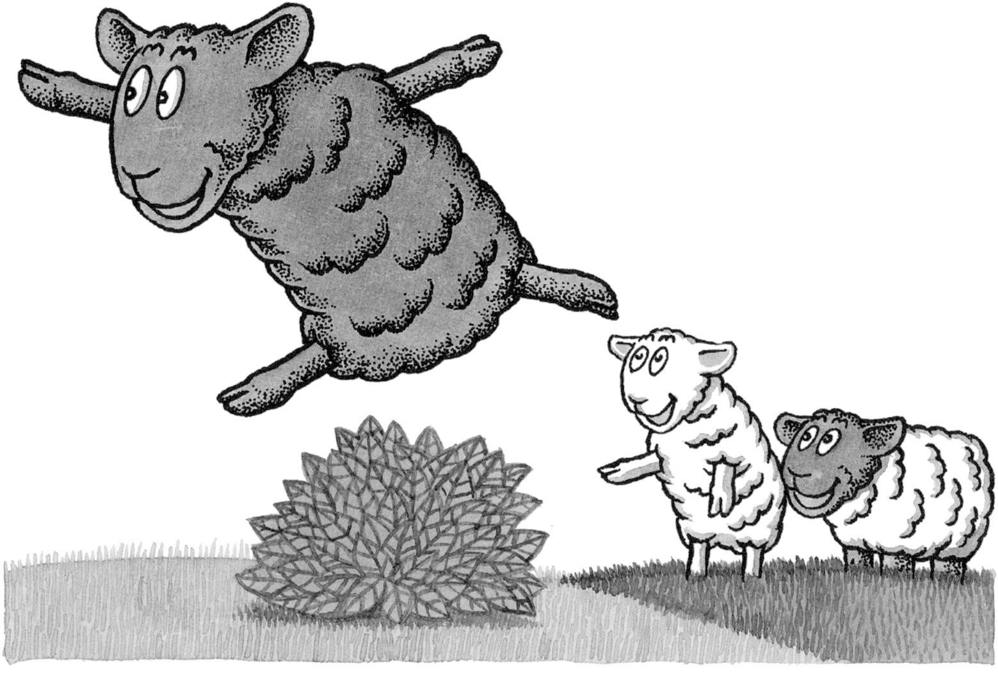

Max jumps over a fence.

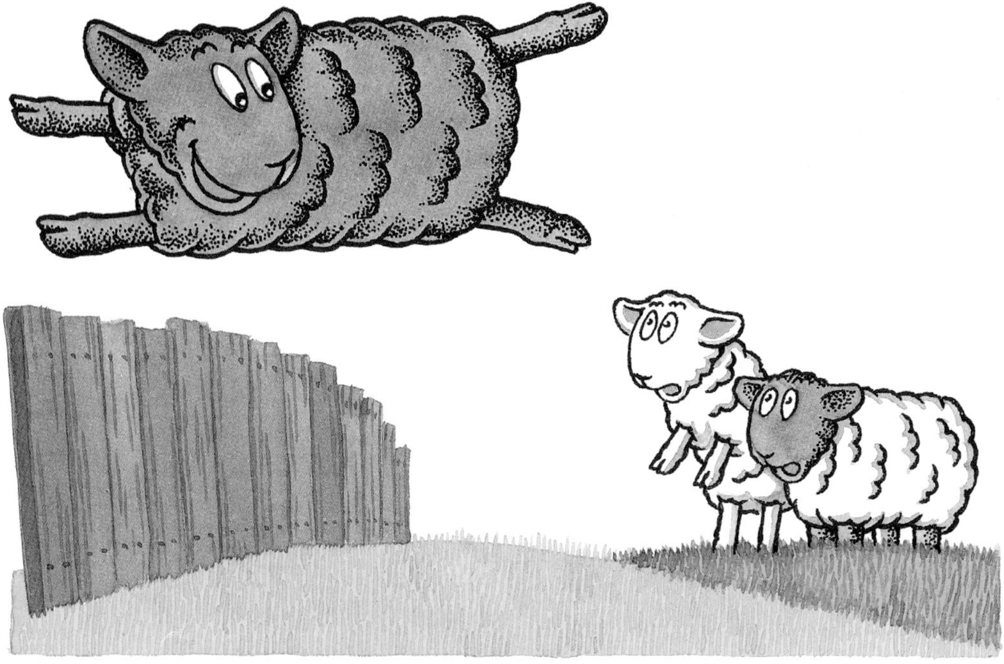

Max jumps over a hedge.

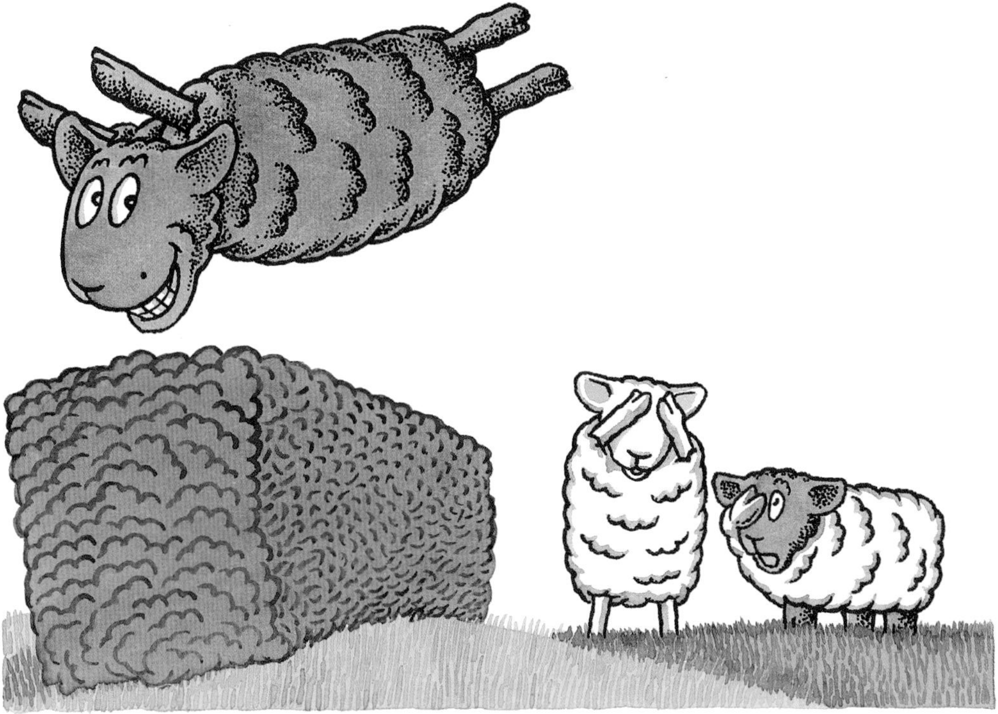

Oh no!

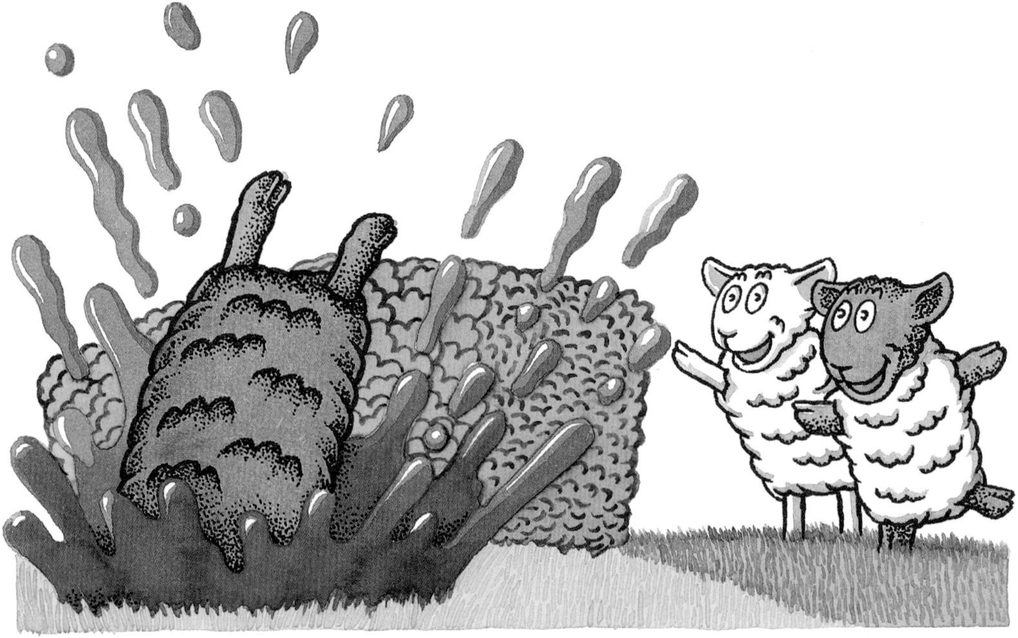